The Dog Lover's Cookbook

The Dog Lover's Cookbook:
Dr. Tonken's Book of Practical Canine Cuisine

Bernard Tonken, DVM.

Illustrated by Don Inman

THE MAIN STREET PRESS
Pittstown, New Jersey

This book is dedicated to my wife, Lil, whose continuous encouragement stimulated me to write it, and to her dog, Farrah, who was good enough to taste test the recipes.

All rights reserved

Copyright © 1985, 1987 by Bernard Tonken, DVM

No part of this book may be utilized or reproduced in any form or by any means, electronic or mechanical, including photocopying, recording, or by any information storage and retrieval system, without permission in writing from the publishers.

Published by
The Main Street Press
William Case House
Pittstown, New Jersey 08867

Published simultaneously in Canada by
Methuen Publications
2330 Midland Avenue
Agincourt, Ontario M1S 1P7

Printed in the United States of America

Library of Congress Cataloging-in-Publication Data

Tonken, Bernard
  The dog lover's cookbook.

  Includes index.
  1. Dogs—Food—Recipes. I. Title
SF427.4.T66 1987 636.7'085 87-20417
ISBN 1-55562-034-5 (pbk.)

TABLE OF CONTENTS

Foreword   7

Introduction to Canine Cuisine   9

GENERAL INFORMATION   12

COMMON INGREDIENTS USED IN CANINE COOKING   25

SOUPS   36

SANDWICHES   41

ALL-DAY BREAKFASTS   44

MAIN COURSES (ENTRÉES)   49

COOKIES   62

THE DELICATE ART OF COOKING ORGANS   66

FEEDING THE SICK ANIMAL   75

PREGNANT BITCHES, NURSING BITCHES, AND ORPHAN PUPPIES   91

THE OVERWEIGHT PROBLEM: RECIPES FOR THE OBESE DOG   100

MEALS ON WHEELS: FEEDING THE OLDER DOG   107

FEEDING THE WORKING DOG   115

CATERING FOR A CROWD   120

Table of Equivalents and Conversions   125

Index   126

FOREWORD

It was with some trepidation that we took it upon ourselves to write and publish what is probably the only dog cookbook in existence today. It took years for someone to be brave enough to do it.

Critics will tell us that a dog should be fed the same commercial brand of food day after day. We will reply that, yes, that is one way—but there can be another.

No one will argue that a dog is a companion. The word is derived from the Latin "com" meaning "with" and "panis" meaning "bread": a bread fellow or messmate. My dog, who spends most of her day at my side, shares my food.

This is a serious book, written and illustrated on the light side. The recipes are ones that I, my wife, my mother, and others have used over the years. As with human recipes, some your dog will enjoy, others she won't.

INTRODUCTION TO CANINE CUISINE

My dog is one of the family and she'll eat anything as long as it isn't dog food.

She must have read the bible in her other life—Matthew XV, verse 27: "The dogs eat of the crumbs which fall from their master's table." Most of the recipes in this book are meant for dogs, but there are some that you can eat, too! It depends on your frame of mind and your outlook on life.

Your dog counts on you to provide a tasty, nutritionally adequate diet. Take away the boredom of the same meal day after day with recipes that are healthy, economical, and fun to make. You can feed them right from the oven, or mix them with the dog food that you're presently buying.

Various sections included in this book

contain recipes not only for the normal healthy dog, but for the sick, the overweight, the working dog, the aged dog, the pregnant female, the orphan pup, and the growing pup.

The feeding and care of your pet is a pleasant responsibility. Know that you could be making one of your family happy today.

GENERAL INFORMATION

THE DOG'S DIET

A balanced ration includes protein, carbohydrates, fat, vitamins, and minerals—all in their proper proportions. Most foods contain these ingredients in varying quality and quantity. Energy, which is also derived from the food, is a fundamental requirement.

In order for you to keep the diet reasonably balanced, you should understand the quality and quantity of the various ingredients in the different foods your recipes will contain.

You'll have no problem using the recipes in this book, and with them, creating some yourself. All that you need is that basic understanding of what you should normally feed dogs.

Protein

The primary use for this substance is tissue building. It should not have to be called on for energy. High quality proteins are found in meat, milk, eggs, and some plants.

Carbohydrates

Carbohdrates account for 60% to 70% of the dog's diet. This substance, which is converted to energy, is found in good quality and quantity in cereals, rice, and bread.

Fat

Fat is the dog's major source of energy. Proper amounts are required for a normal skin and beautiful coat. The best source is bacon fat or vegetable oil. For the dog, beef fat is not complete, and rancid fat can be harmful.

Vitamins and Minerals

These are essential for some of the life processes. Along with vitamin D, calcium and phosphorous in the ratio of 1.2 to 1 are critical. The necessary requirement is supplied by many foods, including vegetables. You may purchase supplements if necessary, but they should not be used indiscriminately.

Salt

Iodized salt is the product of choice, but should always be used in moderation. It is said that as long as water is freely available, you probably will never be able to give your dog too much salt.

Water

Water is an essential part of the dog's diet, and should always be clean and freely available.

Vegetables

Stay away from peas and beans. Use items like carrots, celery, and lettuce. Potatoes, along with their peels, can be added to the vegetables. Make this group of low-cost foods a nutritious part of your dog's diet.

Vegetables can be fed raw or cooked. The shorter the cooking time, the better the nutritional value and the more interesting the flavor. Fry them or steam them, but don't drown them in a pot of water. If you must boil them, save the cooking water for soups and broths.

KINDS OF FOODS USED IN CANINE COOKING

Meat

Dogs are carnivorous, but believe it or not, they cannot function properly on a diet of 100% meat. The acceptable level is about 50% of the diet.

Although dogs will eat any kind of meat, certain meats are more nutritious than others. Except for pork and rabbit, meat can be fed raw, although cooking is preferable.

Common meats used are beef, veal, pork, mutton, rabbit, horseflesh, and wild game. The organs of animals are excellent meat foods. Recipes can include lung, liver, heart, brain, spleen, kidney, and sweetbreads.

Try to avoid processed, highly spiced meat such as salami and garlic rings.

Fish

You can use fish frequently, but it must always be cooked and the bones removed. Fish meal is a common ingredient of many commercial dog foods.

Eggs

Eggs are an easily digested, valuable food that is best fed cooked. Mix eggs with other foods and use them to replace some of the meat in the diet. Dogs don't mind brown eggs or blood spots—so why not buy these cheaper ones for them?

Milk and Cheese

Except for newborn pups, cow's milk is fine to use. Too much milk in the diet can cause diarrhea. If your dog likes cheese, by all means use it. Uncreamed cottage cheese is a favorite.

Cereals

Some commercial dog foods consist almost entirely of grain. It is preferable not to use more than 50% in the ration. This group of foods includes breakfast cereals, white or whole-wheat bread, white or whole-wheat flour, white rice, and brown rice. I have used combinations of white and whole wheat. Always cook cereals before feeding.

People Food

Feeding dogs our own food is a problem for the pet-food industry. We are bombarded with advertisements that tend to suggest that pet food is better than table scraps—which of course is our food. Think about it. It's ludicrous to throw away our leftovers and go out and buy dog food as a replacement. Recipes in the book will give you ideas on how to use and feed people food.

Commercial Dog Food

AN APPRAISAL

Until about 125 years ago, dogs ate whatever they could get, plus a diet of table scraps. Then the first dog food appeared on the market. Today the choice being offered is staggering.

Commercial dog foods have now evolved into five main categories:

DRY DOG FOOD

This food is usually made up of cereal grains, flavoring, vitamins, and minerals.

CANNED DOG FOOD

There are many varieties, including meat, meat and cereal mix, and flavored cereal usually mixed with vegetables.

SEMI-MOIST FOODS

Most often these are combinations of cereals, sugar, and flavoring.

SPECIAL DIETS

These foods are sold canned or dry and are designed for sick dogs with specific problems.

And Now, Nutritious Home-Cooked Foods

Cooking for your dog can be economical, nutritious, and fun to do. That's what this book is all about. Some of the foods can be used as complete diets by themselves, but most of the time you'll be mixing the recipes with other foods that you are presently purchasing.

Whether you cook for your dog or not, you will be buying some pet food. Watch out—like most other things, you get what you pay for. Our laws attempt to protect the consumer, dogs included. Read the label and understand that if it reads:

- "Beef"—and nothing else, the can must contain at least 95% beef.

- "Beef Dinner"—the can must contain at least 25% beef.

- "Beef Flavor"—it doesn't have to have any beef, just taste like it.

- "Complete and Balanced"—must contain all the nutrients required by your dog, in the proper amounts and in a balanced manner.

- "Ingredient List"—in decreasing order and with the largest percentages first, it lists what you are buying. You are probably getting more for your money if the list starts with beef or beef by-products. Note the water content of canned food. It should be about 75%.

When feeding your dog, you can use various combinations of commercial dog foods, fish, table scraps, cereals, vegetables, and home cooking recipes. You can mix moist food or dry food with home recipes.

Some rules of thumb for mixing recipes with other foods:

- Use no more than 25% table scraps in the diet.

- Use no more than 50% meat over long periods of time.

- Use no more than 70% carbohydrates (bread, grains) over long periods.

- When mixing home recipes with commercial dog food, use 50% of each by weight.

When you decide to change your dog's food, always take three or four days to complete the change. Mixing some of the new food with the old on a gradual basis will prevent any stomach or intestinal upsets.

AMOUNT TO FEED

The individual requirement will vary from dog to dog. Even dogs of the same weight will eat different amounts in a given day. The proper amount to feed is the amount necessary to maintain body weight and condition. If your dog gains or loses more than 5% of its body weight, you should adjust the amount that you are feeding.

For mature dogs, the average food consumption is:

- Dry commercial dog foods—
  1 cup per 10 lbs body weight per day.
- Canned dog food—1¼ oz per pound of body weight per day
- Home-cooked recipes—1¼ oz per pound of body weight per day.
- Mixture of home-cooked recipes and dry dog food—1 oz per pound of body weight per day.

COMMON INGREDIENTS USED IN CANINE COOKING

RICE

Use white or brown. Rinse one cup in cold water to remove the dust.

Put rice into cooking pot and add 1¾ cups of cold water. Salt to taste and stir well.

Bring to a boil and allow to simmer under a tight lid. Simmer white rice for 15 minutes and brown rice for 25 minutes.

Turn off the heat and allow rice to cool, leaving pot on burner.

NOTES:

Unused rice should be refrigerated. When reheating, add 2 tablespoons of water in order to keep the rice moist.

One cup of raw rice will make about 3 cups of cooked rice.

When cooking rice or grains, to enhance the taste, use a broth instead of water. You can make a broth by adding one level teaspoon of chicken- or beef-flavored soup base for every cup of water used in the recipe.

CEREAL GRAINS

Add 1¾ cups of cold water to a cooking pot and salt to taste.

Slowly stir in 1 cup of cereal or mixed cereal grains.

Bring to a boil and simmer with a tight lid for 15 minutes. Allow to cool.

Like rice, cereals may be refrigerated for next-day use. When reheating, add 2 tablespoons of water in order to keep cereal moist.

VEGETABLES

You can pan fry by adding 2 tablespoons of vegetable oil to a frying pan and heating. Add the desired amount of raw chopped vegetables to the hot pan and stir fry for 10 minutes.

To steam cook, add ¼ inch of water to a cooking pot and salt to taste. Bring to a boil, add chopped vegetables, and simmer for 20 minutes. Drain the water and save for future use as a broth.

CEREAL RICE MIX

A Favorite Additive

Add 2 cups of cold water or broth to a cooking pot and salt to taste.

Slowly mix in ⅔ of a cup of white rice and ⅓ of a cup of cereal grain.

Bring to a boil and allow to simmer with a tight lid for 15 minutes. Allow to cool.

Use desired amount in recipe and refrigerate unused portion. When reheating, add 2 tablespoons of water in order to keep moist.

NOTES:

When mixing rice or grains with canned dog food, use cans that contain all meat, and mix 50% by weight of each.

Another good combination is a mixture of 50% rice or grain, 25% table scraps, and 25% canned meat dog food.

MEAT

These are pointers to remember:

- Less tender cuts are as nutritious as the more expensive cuts.

- Ground meats and organ meats should be cooked within 24 hours of purchasing. If you intend to store the meat for more than two days, freeze it.

- When roasting meat, roast in a slow oven at 300°F (150°C). Always place the meat fat side up in the roaster.

- The average roast, if baked in an oven at 325°F (160°C), will take 35 minutes per pound to cook.

- When cooking or roasting wild game, where possible remove the fat and bones first. This will help remove the wild taste.

THE DOS AND DON'TS OF FEEDING AS WELL AS OTHER THINGS

Rabbit or pork should not be fed unless thoroughly cooked.

Fish should never be fed raw; once it is cooked, remove the bones.

Fresh water should always be available and fed from a clean bowl.

Never overfeed. The right amount is usually what the dog will eat in about fifteen minutes. Some dogs will save portions of their food for later.

When you reduce the volume of food, you may want to consider using vitamin-mineral supplements.

Overfeeding is more harmful than underfeeding.

It doesn't hurt to serve a large dog his meals on a one-foot-high box.

When using vegetable oil or bacon fat, use, as a rule of thumb, one-half to one teaspoon per pound of food.

A beaten egg means that the yolk and white are blended.

Be consistent in the number of times per day, as well as the time of day, that you feed your animal.

I believe that the self-feeding system should be restricted to kennels, puppies, or poor doers.

Don't feed table scraps to your puppy. When the dog matures, use the scraps but mix them with other foods.

Feed dog food at room temperature or warmer, and not directly from the refrigerator.

If a dog is "off" his food, try some canned chicken cat food. Feed at room temperature or warmer.

Soy milk is becoming fashionable and it won't hurt your dog.

Occasionally I give my dog cooked potato peels and I haven't hurt her yet.

If you talk to your butcher he'll save you scraps and fresh organ meats at bargain prices.

Yes, you can use a little buttermilk now and then.

Always remove bones from the food.

Give your dog long, flat bones to chew on or substitute with commercial leather bones.

Know that you have a problem if the dog trains you, instead of you training the dog.

It is better to cook the vegetables than to feed them raw. It is even better to fry them than cook them.

Use raw eggs only occasionally. Cook most eggs before feeding.

Lettuce, raw or boiled, can be used in the dog's food.

Disposable diapers make good bedding for old dogs or for females with pups.

If you buy only one kind of dry dog food, grind it in a blender when you want a dog meal.

Chicken soup, with or without noodles, may not help, but it won't hurt.

An occasional quarter cup of raisins in a recipe might be interesting.

If you are going to change your dog's diet, do it over a three- to four-day span.

Liver is great for dogs, but too much of it can have a laxative effect.

Spleen is a cheap, nutritious, organ food and should be treated the same as liver.

Cook quantities of food at one time. Package it in the amount fed daily and freeze for future use.

In many recipes, instead of flour, you can use rolled oats or corn meal.

We don't know for sure to what degree dogs taste, but we do know for sure that they discriminate among the various foods.

If you use dry skim-milk powder in the food, use up to 5%.

In normal, healthy dogs, the nutritional requirements can be met by improving the quality of the food, as well as the amount.

One pound of carrots, when diced, will equal four cups.

Before buying a commercial dog food, read the label.

Always cook cereals before feeding.

If you have to give your dog a pill, feed him a quarter teaspoon of peanut butter first, then repeat with the pill in it.

SOUPS

BEEF TEA

In a large glass bowl, place

1 lb fresh raw lean minced meat
16 oz cold water
½ teaspoon iodized salt

Stir to break up the beef and soak overnight in the refrigerator.

Next morning simmer for 1 hour and then strain through a wire strainer.

Add enough water to strained liquid to bring to 16 oz.

Feed the meat in the strainer mixed with equal amounts of dry dog food.

Feed the tea warm, especially if guests are present. Tea can also be used to moisten dog foods in order to increase palatability.

OCEAN BROTH

If you ask the owner of your local fish market, he might give you 1 lb of discarded fish bones, heads, skin and tails.

Add the fish to 1 quart of cold water and salt to taste.

Bring to a boil and simmer for 2 hours.

Chop and add—1 large carrot
                      1 small parsnip
                      1 stalk celery

Simmer for 30 more minutes.

Strain through a fine strainer.

Allow to cool to warm, and feed. Leftover broth can be frozen for future use.

Should you attempt to pick out the vegetables, make sure you discard the bones.

MOTHER'S MEAT SOUP

Use: 2 lbs raw bones, beef or poultry or any combination of them.
2 quarts cold water
¼ teaspoon salt
parsley flakes
2 medium-sized carrots
2 stalks celery
1 small onion
1 small parsnip

Add the meat, bones, and cold water to a large cooking pot. Add the salt, a touch of parsley, bring to a boil, and simmer for 3 hours.

Add chopped-up vegetables and simmer for another 30 minutes.

Let cool to room temperature.

Strain and discard bones, but keep any meat and vegetables.

Refrigerate soup and the next day spoon off excess fat.

Feed soup warm. Use to moisten other foods as well.

Feed the vegetable-meat portions. Freeze excess soup.

MIXED VEGETABLE SOUP

This economical broth is made by using:
- 1 small onion
- 2 stalks celery
- 2 medium-sized carrots
- 1 medium-sized parsnip
- ¼ cup barley

Add all ingredients to a pot containing 1 quart of water. Salt to taste.

Bring to a boil and simmer for 1 hour.

Allow to cool to warm, and feed.

Vegetables may be strained off and mixed with other foods.

Freeze excess broth for future use.

SANDWICHES

THE LIVER BEST

(A Liver and Egg Combo)

Soak 8 oz of freshly sliced liver in one beaten egg.

Place one slice of bread on a greased pan.

Place liver slices on bread and pour egg over it.

Cover with second slice of bread.

Mix 1 cup water with 1 tablespoon enriched white flour and pour over sandwich.

Cover and bake at 300°F (150°C) for 1 hour.

Allow to cool and feed.

THE DOGHOUSE

(A Canine Denver)

Use: 1 lb of fresh tripe
 1 raw egg
 ½ cup milk
 3 slices bread

If you can't get a pound of tripe free, buy it. Wash tripe with cold water and cut into rectangular pieces.

Grease a pan and place 1 slice of bread on it.

Place tripe pieces on bread and pour ½ a beaten egg over tripe.

Place a second slice of bread on egg and top with more tripe. Salt to taste and add third slice of bread.

Moisten entire sandwich with ½ cup of milk and cover pan.

Bake for 1 hour at 300°F (150°C).

Allow to cool and feed this nutritious, delicious delicacy.

ALL-DAY BREAKFASTS

BACON 'N' EGGS BREADED

(For You or Your Dog)

Fry 3 slices of bacon to a crisp and then chop.

Mix the bacon with ½ cup of soft bread crumbs.

Leave the drippings from the bacon in the pan and add the bread-crumb mix to it. Heat until crumbs are crisp and brown. Remove from pan.

Mix together ¼ cup of milk and 2 well-beaten eggs. Salt to taste. (If you're going to have some, add a dash of pepper as well.)

Pour back into same pan and scramble until nearly set.

Add crumb mix to pan with eggs.

Cool to warm and share with dog. If you have a big dog, double the ingredients so dog will get enough.

RALPH'S GRILL

Pour ½" broth into a frying pan.

Add 8 oz. of chopped raw meat or last night's beef leftovers. No bones.

Salt to taste and bring to a boil. Simmer for 5 minutes.

Add 1 fresh egg and mix contents without beating.

Heat for 5 more minutes.

Allow to cool and mix with dry dog meal or cooked rice in 50% proportions.

LIVER OMELET

Lightly fry 4 oz. of chopped liver in a hot greased pan.

Beat 2 eggs and add to liver.

Fry lightly and turn. Continue frying until set.

Cut into pieces and mix until blended with cooked rice or dry dog food in 50% proportions.

SCRAPPY OMELET

Add 2 tablespoons of vegetable oil to a pan and heat.

Chop 4 oz of meat scraps and fry.

Beat 2 eggs gently and pour over meat in pan. Fry until eggs are set.

Cut into small pieces and mix with equal quantities of cooked cereal grains or dry commercial dog food.

LAYER CAKE

Cover the bottom of a greased pan with 2 sliced hard-boiled eggs.

Spread 2 oz chopped raw meat or hamburger over eggs.

Place more egg slices over meat. Add 2 oz more meat.

Add just enough water to cover and bake at 300°F (150°C) for 1 hour.

Mix with an equal volume of dog meal or cooked rice and feed.

THE SCATTERBRAIN

(A Fried Brain Omelet)

Wash fresh brain with cold water and drain. Chop into small chunks.

Beat 2 raw eggs and mix well with one tablespoon of enriched white flour.

Blend brains, eggs, and flour together.

Fry mixture in oiled hot pan for 2 minutes on each side .

Allow to cool and mix with equal parts commercial dry dog food. Refrigerate unused omelet for next day's use.

MAIN COURSES (ENTRÉES)

SAUSAGE ON SALE

Use: 1 lb sausage meat
      1 egg
      2 cups cornflakes

Make 6 sausage patties.

Beat egg and mix with 3 tablespoons of water.

Place cornflakes in shallow pan.

Dip patties in egg and then roll in cornflakes.

Fry slowly, browning both sides until done.

Allow patties to cool. Feed by mixing with equal amounts by weight of either dry crumbled stale bread or dry commercial dog food.

DACHSHUND WIENERS

Split 2 wieners lengthwise and place in a shallow pan.

Pile 2 cups of mashed potatoes on wieners.

Sprinkle ¼ cup of grated cheese over potatoes.

Bake for 20 minutes at 400°F (200°C) and feed warm.

BASEBALLS

Combine: ½ cup raw white rice
1 lb. of ground beef
1 teaspoon salt
1 teaspoon minced onion

Shape into 10 or 12 balls.

Spread 2 tablespoons of vegetable oil in a frying pan and heat. Brown the balls in the pan and then add water.

Cover and cook until the rice is tender—about 1½ hours at 300°F (150°C).

Allow to cool. Feed as is or mix with 25% dry dog food. Freeze unused portions for future use.

THE ENERGIZER

(A High-Protein Hash)

Mix equal parts of lean, raw or cooked chopped meat with crumbled stale bread.

Add one chopped hard-boiled egg and salt to taste.

Moisten with a little warm milk and feed.

STANDARD FAST FOOD

Mix ½ can of dog food with leftover table scraps. Add dog meal or cooked rice equal by weight to the dog food and scraps used.

Moisten with a small quantity of warm milk or broth.

Feed warm so dog will think you ordered in.

MACARONI 'N' CHEESE

(Use When You Forget to Buy Rice)

Cook 6 oz. of macaroni using directions given on box.

Mix ½ cup of cubed light cheese into macaroni.

Add ½ teaspoon of salt and 1¼ cups of milk. Mix lightly.

Place in a casserole dish and bake for 45 minutes at 350°F (175°C).

Let cool and mix with meat scraps or hamburger in amounts equal to the quantities of macaroni used.

COMPLETE MACARONI DINNER

Cut up celery and carrots to make up ⅓ of a cup of each.

Add 2 tablespoons of vegetable oil to a hot pan and fry the celery and carrots until they are partially cooked.

Add 12 oz of either diced meat, meat scraps, or hamburger and cook lightly in the same pan with the vegetables.

Add 2½ cups of water to the frying pan. Mix well and let simmer for 30 minutes.

Cook raw macaroni for 7 minutes in boiling salted water and drain.

Place half the amount of macaroni that dog will eat at this meal in dog's bowl and top with an equal amount of fried vegetables and meat.

Mix well and feed warm to dog. Freeze leftovers for future use.

MEAN CUISINE

(Not to be Confused with Diet Products)

Combine the following ingredients and mix lightly:
- 1 cup cooked macaroni
- ¼ cup grated cheese
- 1 cup of milk
- 1 cup of bread crumbs
- 2 beaten eggs
- ¼ teaspoon salt
- 1 cup chopped meat

Pour mixture into a greased baking dish and bake at 325°F (160°C) for 1 hour.

Cool to a warm temperature and feed. Freeze leftovers for future use. This total recipe has about 1450 calories.

A STANDARD MEAL

For normal, healthy adult dogs, equal parts of raw or cooked meat, mixed with cereal grains or bread and warmed with broth, may be fed. If used often, add vitamin-mineral supplements.

POKER NIGHT PIG-OUT

When You're in a Real Hurry—

Quickly open a 14-oz can of spaghetti.

Drain the tomato sauce and replace it with an equal amount of water.

Pour the spaghetti and water into a baking pan.

Add about 6 oz of hot dogs or chopped-up meat table scraps.

If you have time, add ¼ cup of chopped raw celery. If you don't have time, break up one slice of bread and use it, but feed the celery tomorrow.

Heat mixture by baking or cooking,

Feed warm. Dog may hate you for it, but at least she will have been fed.

CHOPPED LIVER TREAT

(A Healthy Handout Between Meals)

Ingredients:
- 8 ounces of beef liver
- 2 hard-boiled eggs
- 1 ounce of chopped onion

Sauté the liver, and salt to taste. Now sauté the onions to a light brown.

Cut up the liver and the eggs and then put the liver, eggs, and onions through a meat grinder.

After grinding, use a wooden bowl to chop it up again. While chopping, add enough vegetable oil to moisten well.

Feed as treats or add 2 ounces to main meals. Refrigerate unused portions.

NOTE:

You may use this recipe for hors d'oeuvres at your next party. Feed the leftover to the dog.

TRIPE TREAT

Rinse 1 pound of fresh tripe in cold water and drain.

Place in a pot, cover with fresh water, and salt to taste.

Bring to a boil and simmer for 1 hour.

Drain and cut into 2-inch pieces.

Beat 1 egg and combine with an equal amount of water.

Dip tripe first into egg mixture and then into a bowl of dry bread crumbs.

Fry pieces in a hot greased pan and brown on both sides.

You can feed tripe treat alone or mix with other foods. The best mix is $\frac{1}{3}$ tripe to $\frac{2}{3}$ of other dog foods. Refrigerate for future use.

GERMAN SHEPHERD MEAT PIE

Get ready:
- 6 ounces of broth
- 8 ounces of meat scraps
- 1 cup of whole-wheat flour
- 8 ounces of dog meal

Grease a pan and spread half the meat in it.

Sprinkle the meat generously with whole-wheat flour.

Spread remaining half of meat into pan and salt to taste.

Sprinkle again with whole-wheat flour.

Cover with 8 ounces of dog meal and pour broth over the meal.

Bake at 300°F (150°C) for 45 minutes and then allow to cool.

Feed warm.

CHUCKWAGON STEW

Cut 1 pound of meat into small chunks of about 1 inch in size.

Dip the meat into the flour and brown on all sides in a hot pan.

Salt to taste and add enough hot water to barely cover the meat.

Cover pan with a tight lid and simmer until meat is almost tender.

Add a 1-pound mix of freshly chopped vegetables (carrots, celery, parsnip).

Cube one whole potato and add to pan.

Simmer for another 30 minutes and allow to cool.

Feed the desired quantity warm and refrigerate the remainder for tomorrow's use.

LEFTOVER HASH CAKE

Blend a mix of:
- 2 cups of leftover meat scraps
- 2 cups diced cooked potatoes
- 1 teaspoon minced dry onion
- 1 cup of leftover gravy

Pour the blend into a greased pan and spread 2 cups of buttered bread crumbs on top of it.

Bake at 350°F (175°C) for 25 minutes.

Cool to a warm temperature and feed.

SHEEPDOG LAMB STEW

Gather up the leftover lamb and discard most of the fat and all of the bones. Cut into small pieces and place in pan. Cover with water and simmer for 1 hour.

For every pound of leftovers, add ½ cup of raw sliced carrots and 1½ cups of raw cubed potatoes. Salt to taste and simmer for another 30 minutes.

Drain broth. Feed stew mixed with equal amounts of dry dog food.

COWBOY CASSEROLE

This dish is normally fed at rodeo time when the boys can think that the dog is getting their food. Feeding the boys first seems to improve the flavor for the dog.

Into a casserole dish, put:
    1 layer sliced raw potatoes
    1 layer sliced raw carrots
    1 layer ground beef
    Another layer sliced raw potatoes

Sprinkle ¼ cup of raw white rice over layers.

Add another layer of sliced raw potatoes.

Pour 6 oz of water over ingredients and salt to taste.

Bake at 300°F (150°C) for 2½ hours.

Feed hot to the boys. Allow to cool for the dog. Refrigerate leftovers for next day use.

GOURMET CANINE COOKIES

Mix 12 oz of enriched white flour with 3 oz chopped meat scraps.

Add 1 oz of melted fat, roast drippings, or vegetable oil.

Moisten with enough water to give it the consistency you need and roll out to ¼" thickness.

Cut into the cookie shape that your dog most prefers.

Oil a baking sheet and bake at 300°F (150°C) until crisp.

You can feed the cookies whole or crumble them and mix with other food. Unused cookies can be kept in the refrigerator or frozen for future use.

BUSTER'S BAGELS

If you need to impress your dog, but you're too lazy to bake, make a deal with the local supermarket. Offer them $1.00 for a dozen stale bagels. (They will think you're paying too much). Cut them into quarters and let them dry out. Treat them as cookies. The dog will love them and you. Freeze portions for future use if desired.

KIDDIES' COOKIES

Let the kids and the dog watch you bake these. Give them to the ones who have been good.

Use: 5 eggs
½ lb white flour
½ lb white sugar

Beat the eggs and sugar to a cream. Add the flour a little at a time, stirring well. Put on a cookie sheet by the teaspoon and bake at 375°F (190°C) until done.

What you don't give the dog, give to the kids.

SNAPPY BISCUITS

Purchase a stale unsliced whole-wheat bread. Let it go hard.

Cut the stale hard bread into ½" or ¾" slices, then halve and quarter.

Sprinkle the slightest amount of garlic powder onto pieces.

Lay out on a pan and bake at 300°F (150°C) until pieces are crisp.

Store in air-tight containers until used. Feed whole or crumble and mix with other food.

NOTE:

If your dog develops bad breath, eliminate the garlic.

THE DELICATE ART OF COOKING ORGANS

HEARTBREAKERS

Buy some heart—beef, lamb, or pork. Ask the butcher to grind it. Then combine:
  1 lb of ground heart
  1 teaspoon onion flakes
  Salt to taste

Shape into patties and fry in greased hot pan. Brown on both sides.

Feed warm, mixed with equal amounts of dry dog food or cooked rice. Freeze unused portions for future use. Ground heart is not only appetizing, but very healthy.

SPLEEN

This organ has about the same nutritional value as liver. Buy it when you can; it is inexpensive. Use liver recipes to prepare it, in each instance replacing the liver with the spleen.

A BIG-HEARTED RECIPE

Purchase a fresh whole beef heart. Wash in cold water and drain, but do not intentionally remove fat or blood clots.

Fill the cavities with bread crumbs and place in a pot with just enough water to cover.

Salt to taste and simmer for 2 hours.

Add 1 cup of combined cut-up celery and carrots, and simmer for another ½ hour.

Drain, but save the broth. Let the heart cool and cut into chunks.

Feed mixed with some of the vegetables. If desired, you may add to dry dog food.

You can freeze the broth or heart-vegetable mix for future use.

A SMALL-HEARTED RECIPE

Buy a fresh pork or lamb heart. Wash in cold water.

Slit heart halfway open and stuff with bread crumbs.

Place in an open greased pan and bake at 300°F (150°C) for 1 hour.

Allow to cool and cut into chunks.

Can be fed alone or mixed with dry dog food or cooked rice.

BROILED KIDNEYS

Wash kidneys in cold water, split them, and remove fat and visible tubes.

Brush lightly with vegetable oil and salt to taste.

Broil 5 minutes on each side, 7 minutes if they are large.

Serve on dried stale bread or toast. Save extra portions in the refrigerator for tomorrow's feeding.

KIDNEY STEW

Requires:
- 1 beef kidney
- 6 tablespoons white flour
- 1 chopped hard-boiled egg

Wash a fresh kidney and then cut crosswise into ½" slices and then into small pieces.

Soak in cold water for 15 minutes and drain.

Place in cooking pot, add water, bring to a boil, and simmer for 1½ hours without a cover. Let cool.

Mix flour with an equal amount of water and make a paste.

Drain all but 3 cups of liquid from kidney and reheat.

Add flour paste gradually while stirring and cook until thickened. Salt to taste.

Add chopped egg. Mix well.

Feed by mixing with equal amounts by weight of dry dog food or cooked rice.

BOILED BEEF TONGUE

(It Could Leave You Speechless)

Wash and drain a whole fresh beef tongue.

Place in cooking pot with just enough water to cover and bring to a boil.

Simmer for 2 to 3 hours, depending on size of tongue.

Add one cup of a mixture of chopped carrots and celery. Simmer for an additional 30 minutes.

Remove tongue and allow to cool. Peel outside skin and cut excess fat and bone away.

Cut tongue into slices and then pieces.

Feed tongue and vegetables mixed with equal parts by weight of dry dog food or cooked rice.

Freeze unused portions for future use.

SWEETBREADS

(For Dogs on an Expense Account)

Stand the sweetbreads in cold water for 20 minutes, wash, and drain.

Put sweetbreads in a cooking pot with 2 quarts of water. Add 2 tablespoons of vinegar and 1 tablespoon of salt. Mix and bring to a boil.

Simmer for 30 minutes and drain.

Cut into pieces and mix an equal amount by weight of crumbled dry stale bread or dry dog meal with pieces.

Freeze any excess quantities for future use.

HOW TO COOK BRAINS

The brain of any animal can be fed to dogs as long as it is cooked. If you decide that you are eating some of it as well, then for a meal full of thought, follow this simple procedure:

- Cook the brains the same day you purchase them.

- Cover the brains with cold water and add 2 tablespoons of vinegar. Soak for 30 minutes.

- Drain and remove loose membranes.

- Simmer in salted water for 30 minutes.

- Remove brain and chill in cold water. Drain again.

You are now ready to use brain in other recipes.

Breaded Brains

Cut a cooked brain into chunks.

Dip chunks into a beaten egg and then into bread crumbs.

Grease a pan with vegetable oil and fry brains to the liking of you and your dog.

Scrambled Brains

Chop cooked brains into small pieces and fry in butter.

Add beaten eggs and scramble.

Eat hot. If you give some to the dog, let cool and mix with dry dog food.

Floured Brains

Cut cooked brain into medium-sized pieces and just cover with water.

Add ¼ cup white flour and simmer for 20 minutes.

Drain and mix with equal amounts by weight of any dry dog food or stale crumbled bread.

FEEDING THE SICK ANIMAL

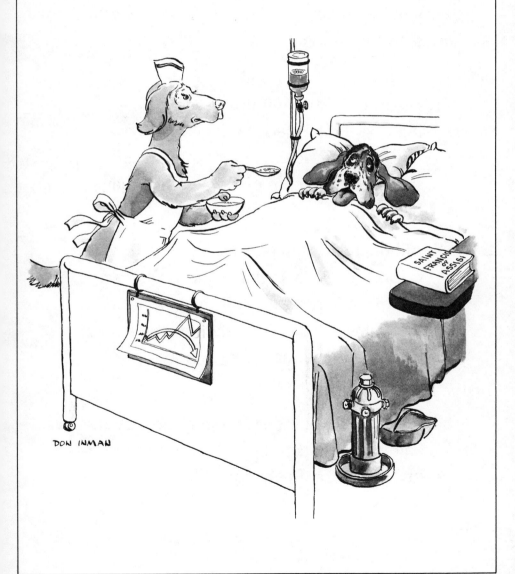

Sick animals, like sick people, require special diets. That is why hospitals that treat humans employ full-time dieticians to look after the nutritional needs of each patient. An animal will recover only as well as his nutritional status will permit.

This section of the book is devoted exclusively to the nutritional care of the ailing dog. Proper feeding is a valuable adjunct to your veterinarian's therapy and should not be considered as a treatment by itself.

Although sick animals do not usually burn calories through exercise, their caloric requirements increase with the severity of their illness. During disease afflictions, the vitamin-mineral daily requirement probably increases as well.

Water is the nutrient required most by the animal and except in the control of vomiting should be freely available.

HEART DISEASE

Dogs afflicted with heart problems should be restricted to diets containing:
- High protein
- High carbohydrates
- Low fat
- Low sodium

Foods that fit this category, and should be included in your recipes, are:
- Boiled meat or poultry
- Custard or skim-milk pudding
- Frozen vegetables
- Potatoes
- Cooked rice or cooked dry cereals
- Unsalted butter or unsalted vegetable oils
- Vitamin-mineral supplements

Do not use leftover broths

Eliminate:
- Snacks
- Treats
- Table scraps
- Salt

Typical Recipe for Heart Disease

Mix:
- 8 oz fresh lean beef, boiled and chopped
- 2 cups of cooked rice
- 1 teaspoon corn oil
- A balanced vitamin-mineral supplement

Mix all the ingredients well and feed warm. Save the unused portions in the refrigerator for use the next day.

If a low-calcium diet is being fed continuously, add one teaspoon dicalcium phosphate to the food daily.

Throughout the chapters of this book, you will find recipes containing the foods prescribed for heart disease diets. Use some of these, but remember to eliminate all salt and not to use the broth.

IF YOUR ANIMAL SUFFERS FROM HEART DISEASE:

Let your veterinarian make the diagnosis.

Don't keep your dog where it may be too hot or too cold.

Make sure the food is palatable.

The drinking water, as well as the food, should be sodium free. If your water softener system utilizes sodium, you may have to use other water for drinking.

Reduce the exercise almost to the point of cage rest.

Give medications you may be using as directed.

STOMACH AND INTESTINAL DISORDERS

Gastrointestinal problems, including vomiting and diarrhea, require bland, nutritious recipes that are low in fiber and have easily digested proteins. Always supplement these recipes with the B complex group of vitamins.

Dogs with stomach and bowel disorders are usually reluctant to eat. Make the food appetizing by following these simple rules:

- Feed the meals at room temperature and not warmed.
- Feed in small amounts four to six times per day.
- Restrict the water intake. Use cold water only. A bowl of ice cubes to lick is a good water substitute.
- For quality protein, use eggs, cottage cheese, and glandular organs.
- Try to include cooked cereals and vitamin B complex supplements.

A Simple Bland Recipe

Mix:

   Bland baby food

   1 chopped hard-boiled egg

   2 oz fresh beef liver

   1 teaspoon white sugar

Use enough baby food to be able to make one day's feeding. Feed equal portions 4 times daily at room temperature.

Another Bland Recipe

Cook enough Cream of Wheat, using package directions, to make 2 cups. To it add:

   1 chopped hard-boiled egg

   ½ cup creamed cottage cheese

   2 oz fresh raw beef liver

   1 teaspoon white sugar

   1 teaspoon corn oil

If your dog doesn't like cheese, replace it with cooked fish.

Divide the day's meal into equal portions and feed four times per day. Refrigerate unused portions for next day.

Remember to supplement bland recipes with B complex vitamins.

KIDNEY DISEASE

This condition can be a complex problem that will require palatable food. If the condition is chronic, you should be feeding normal amounts of protein. If the condition is acute, high levels of protein will be used.

In either case, the carbohydrates should be easily digestible, the fat content about 5%, and the vitamins used should be high in the B complex group.

Your various food choices consist of:
- Eggs
- Cottage cheese
- Liver, kidney, or hamburger
- Cooked rice or cereal grains
- Corn oil
- B complex vitamins

Feed the sick animal small amounts, four to six times per day. Salt your recipes in order to increase consumption of water.

Recipe for Acute Kidney Disease

Pan fry 8 oz. of lean ground beef. Mix with:
- 2 cups cooked white rice
- 3 slices of stale white bread
- 1 chopped hard-boiled egg

Dampen mixture with a little water and salt to taste. Add vitamin-mineral supplements.

Divide into equal portions, and feed small amounts several times daily.

Recipe for Chronic Kidney Disease

Use the same recipe as for acute kidney disease, but use 4 oz of beef instead of 8.

If you use this ration for extended periods of time, supplement twice per week with the addition of 2 oz of lightly fried liver and 1 teaspoon of calcium carbonate.

SKIN AND COAT PROBLEMS

Dog fanciers are well aware that the condition of the skin and hair usually reflects the general health of the animal. If the problem is not of parasitic or allergic origin, there are recipes that can be of help.

For skin conditions including abnormal shedding, the diet should include:

- High levels of protein
- Adequate amounts of carbohydrates
- Moderate amounts of fat
- Vitamin-mineral supplements

Typical Recipe

Mix:

    4 oz raw or cooked hamburger
    1 chopped hard-boiled egg
    1 tablespoon corn oil
    1 cup cooked white rice

Salt to taste and supplement with vitamins and minerals. If the same recipe is fed over long periods, add 2 oz each of cooked carrots and cooked celery.

DIABETES

This complicated disease requires a ration of more protein and less fat than normal. Your veterinarian may prescribe pancreatic enzyme powder as a supplement to your recipes.

Animals suffering from this disease should be fed two to four times per day in moderate amounts. Skim-milk powder along with vitamin-mineral supplements are added to most recipes for diabetic dogs.

Diabetic Diet

Mix:
- 4 oz of lightly boiled lean ground beef
- 2 cups of cooked white rice

To the mixture, add:
- ¼ cup chopped cooked carrots
- ¼ cup cooked green beans
- ½ teaspoon skim-milk powder
- Prescribed amounts of vitamin-mineral supplement.

Mix well and feed warm.

STRESS

In dogs, stress is usually caused by abnormal physical conditions such as accidents or surgery. Long trips or changes in environment can also create stress.

Affected animals should receive 10% to 20% more food than they would be given normally. The meal should be a healthy one, supplemented with tender loving care from you, for the benefit of their mental health.

Stress Recipe

Boil 4 oz of lean hamburger in as little water as possible. Drain and save the liquid.

Mix the hamburger with:
- 1 cup of cooked white rice
- 1 chopped hard-boiled egg

Salt food to taste and moisten with some of the saved liquid. Add a vitamin-mineral supplement as well as one teaspoon of vegetable oil.

Feed warm.

LIVER DISEASE

Hepatic conditions will affect every tissue in the body, and particular attention must be paid to the dog's diet. Recipes should contain:

- Protein in minimal amounts
- Fat in small amounts
- Carbohydrates in high amounts
- Extra amounts of B complex along with vitamins A, D, E, and K.

A Liver Disease Diet

Mix:
    4 oz lean cooked beef
    2 cups cooked white rice
    1 chopped hard-boiled egg
    ½ teaspoon dicalcium phosphate
    Vitamin-mineral supplement high in
        B complex and vitamins A, D, E, and K.

Feed warm and refrigerate unused portions for the next day's feeding.

PROBLEMS AFFECTING THE POSTERIOR THIRD OF THE BODY

Any dog that finds it difficult to pass bowel evacuations requires foods that will be mostly digested. This condition is obvious with a fractured pelvis, a broken hind leg, or diseased anal sacs.

Foods high in fiber should be avoided while the animal is recuperating. Recipes should consist of low fat beef or ground glandular meat, cottage cheese, boiled eggs, and cooked cereals.

A Very Digestible Diet

Mix:
- ½ pound of raw lean beef
- 1 cup cooked white rice
- 1 chopped hard-boiled egg
- Vitamin-mineral supplements

Feed warm and refrigerate unused portions for next day's feeding.

ALLERGY CAUSED BY FOOD

In animals, as in humans, food allergies are becoming common. To correct the condition, it is necessary to identify the food that is the problem and then eliminate it from the diet. In an attempt to make the identification, you will have to feed foods one at a time until you determine the offending one.

One easy way to do this is:

- Feed a diet of equal parts mutton and cooked white rice.
- Add vitamins and minerals according to label directions.
- To this food mix, add, one at a time, foods that you were feeding previously to the dog. By this process of elimination, you should be able to determine the offending one.

GIVING MEDICINES

Medicating your dog is not a difficult procedure.

Liquids:

While the dog is sitting with the head horizontal to the floor, pull out the cheek and let medicine flow into cheek pouch. From there it will drain into the throat.

Pills:

Grasp upper jaw and gently press lips against the teeth. Dog will open his mouth. With your finger, force the pill as far back in the throat as you can. Close dog's mouth so that he will swallow it.

Many liquid medicines and pills have little taste. These may be added to small amounts of food that the dog likes (example—liver or chunks of peanut butter).

PREGNANT BITCHES,

NURSING BITCHES,

AND ORPHAN PUPPIES

PREGNANT AND LACTATING FEMALES

As pregnancy progresses, a bitch will begin consuming about 20% more food than normal. About the fourth week of pregnancy is when the food intake should be increased. Take three or four days to gradually increase the amount of food. To avoid whelping problems, be sure the mother doesn't get too fat.

The diet should be of high quality and include:
- Cooked eggs
- Raw meat
- Milk or milk powder
- Small quantities of liver
- Small quantities of vegetables
- Vitamin-mineral supplements
- Fresh clean water

After the female has had her pups, feed the same ration. It is now that the requirement of vitamins, minerals, and digestible protein increases. As the pups increase in weight, the food intake of the bitch increases proportionately.

Gestation and Lactation Diet

Mix:

    1 pound raw or cooked lean ground or chopped meat

    1 pound of either dog meal, cooked cereal, or crumbled dry bread.

Dampen with warm milk and feed.

Two or three times per week add:

    2 oz cooked vegetables

    2 oz raw or cooked beef liver

    Supplement with vitamins and minerals as necessary.

High Protein Liquid

If the mother seems to be "drained," or she has a large litter, once per week you can make the following mix and give as a noon meal:

Slowly blend:

    8 oz warm milk

    1 raw egg

    2 crushed arrowroot biscuits.

Always feed warm and fresh.

NOTE:

Recipe under stress section of book may be used also.

ORPHAN PUPPIES

Replacements for bitch's milk are simple enough to make, and you should have no problem looking after orphans or runts of the litter.

Your greatest concern will be to neither overfeed nor underfeed. Newborn pups have small stomachs that cannot hold very much. Regular feedings of small amounts many times per day are important. Any changes in amounts fed should be gradual in order to avoid bowel upsets.

When feeding formula, use either a lamb's nipple or a doll's nipple. If neither is available, use an eye dropper.

The amount fed is normally that which the pup will consume in a five to ten minute period. Depending on the breed of dog, this could be about 3 oz per day.

At three weeks of age, puppies should be able to learn to drink milk from a saucer. It is at about this time that you start the pups on some solid food.

Baby foods fed from a saucer work well. The variety that you can purchase is endless, but puppies seem to do best on carrots, beef, and beef and vegetables. At four or five weeks old, begin adding crumbled baby biscuits as well.

Average Number of Times Per Day To Feed Orphan Puppies

Birth to 1 week old—12 times
1 week to 2 weeks old—10 times
2 weeks to 3 weeks old—8 times
3 weeks to 4 weeks old—6 times
4 weeks to 8 weeks old—4 times

Formulas for Orphan, Rejected, or Runt Puppies

GOAT'S MILK

This is the easiest to use and you should be able to buy it in the drug store. This product resembles bitch's milk and requires no modification. Warm milk to body temperature before feeding.

COW'S MILK

Mix 8 ounces of half and half milk (milk and cream) with one egg yolk. Warm to body temperature before feeding.

NOTES:

Always refrigerate unused formula.

Mix new batches every 24 hours.

At 4 weeks old, begin a gradual change to whole cow's milk.

Recipes for Growing Pups

For the first three weeks of the puppy's life, you will be using formula only. Between three and four weeks old, along with the formula, you will start the puppy on solids. At four weeks of age, gradually change from formula to cow's milk and increase the amount of solid food consumed.

The recipes that follow are some that you can use as food solids for young growing puppies.

PUPPY PORRIDGE

Cook breakfast oatmeal porridge and mix with enough warm milk to make a sloppy consistency. Feed warm.

BEEF

Lightly cooked lean beef hamburger can be fed alone. Feed warm.

SLURPY JOE

Use a blender to mix:
- 4 oz warm milk
- 1 scrambled egg
- Enough sliced bread to make a slop.

Feed desired quantity warm.

FISH

Boil fresh fish meat, free of bones, for 10 minutes. Feed warm.

BABY FOODS

If you use them, use the beef and vegetable mix. Baby food can be fed alone or used in other recipes.

Once puppies are eight weeks old, start using soft food recipes. Those that are outlined in this book that are useful include eggs, meat, and cottage cheese, with vitamin-mineral supplements.

And Now Something for the Older Pup

Mix lightly cooked lean beef hamburger or boiled boneless fish with an equal amount of crumbled stale bread. Add one tablespoon of baby food vegetables. Moisten with a little milk and feed warm.

Permanent teeth will begin erupting at about three and a half months old. The permanent teeth will be in place by five and a half months old. For teething, when the puppy needs to chew on something, use flat bones or small commercial rawhide bones.

THE OVERWEIGHT PROBLEM

RECIPES FOR THE OBESE DOG

We aren't the only ones who suffer from overweight problems. Dogs do as well. If you feed more calories than are necessary, you know the end result. Although obesity is most common in older dogs, we have a general tendency to overfeed our pets.

It is much easier to put a dog on a diet than yourself—and the dog can't cheat. Reducing diets should be low in fat, high in protein, and moderate in carbohydrates. During periods of restricted feeding, use a vitamin-mineral supplement and do not allow treats.

Foods that are high in protein and low in fats include cottage cheese, boiled eggs, ground horsemeat, and heart with the fat removed.

Vegetables should supply most of the carbohydrates, especially the leafy green ones. Avoid the peas and beans.

A DIET RECIPE

Use:
- 1 lb cooked ground lean beef
- ½ lb cooked chopped carrots
- ½ lb cooked chopped celery
- 1 chopped hard-boiled egg

Mix all of the above ingredients and supplement with vitamins and minerals.

The above recipe is sufficient to feed a forty-pound dog for one day. In order to avoid hunger pains, divide the food into three equal parts and feed one part every eight hours.

While dogs are on diets, make sure that they receive regular daily exercise.

The amount of exercise will be limited by the physical condition and age of the animal.

ANOTHER DIET RECIPE

Mix:
- 4 oz of ground horsemeat
- or lean ground cooked beef
- ½ cup cottage cheese
- 2 cups sliced cooked carrots
- ½ teaspoon dicalcium phosphate

Divide into two equal portions and feed one portion mid-morning and one during the evening.

This recipe has about 300 calories. A can of dog food has from 500 to 800 calories. For dog's sake, check the calories in this book's tables and try to come up with some of your own recipes.

It might be of interest to check the shelves of your local drugstore. The reducing diets for human use may have a product that can be adapted for dogs. You'll know the calorie count as well.

COUNTING CALORIES

Individual requirements vary from dog to dog and depend on such factors as breed, sex, age, and exercise. A rule of thumb for the average requirement for each twenty-four-hour period is:

Breed	Weight	Calories
Toy breed	5 lbs	225
Small breed	10 lbs	400
Medium size	20 lbs	700
Large size	40 lbs	1200
Larger size	60 lbs	1600
Very large	100 lbs	2400

One can of comercial dog food can vary from 500 calories to 800 calories per can.

TREATS FOR THE OVERWEIGHT DOG

I know, I said no treats, but if you fail this part, it would all have been a waste of time. So if your conscience is going to bother you, use these—

- Allow some cooked or raw vegetables during the day without butter or oil.

- Try some air-popped popcorn, again without butter or oil.

- How about some apple?

- Try some chicken broth without the fat or noodles.

CALORIE CONTENT OF COMMON FOODS FED TO DOGS

1 slice whole-wheat bread	80
1 cup bread crumbs	345
1 cup whole-wheat flour	420
1 cup cooked white rice	200
1 cup noodles	200
1 cup spaghetti	210
1 whole bagel	150
1 cup oatmeal	150
1 doughnut	135
Chicken per oz	35
Bacon per slice	47
Regular hamburger per oz	80
Lean hamburger per oz	61
Beef tongue per oz	69
Pork sausage per oz	136
Sweetbreads per oz	91
Fish per average oz	57
1 cup mashed potatoes	90
1 cup cottage cheese	240
4 oz milk	80
1 oz cheese	100
¼ cup raisins	130
1 tablespoon bacon fat	126
1 tablespoon vegetable oil	125
1 oz sugar	110
1 raw apple	70
1 egg	79
1 cup skim milk	86
1 cup diced celery	5

MEALS ON WHEELS

FEEDING THE OLDER DOG

A DISSERTATION

It's now time to give back some of the care and love that your dog has given you throughout the years. Start by providing a soft warm bed, then concentrate on the diet. Older dogs require less fat, easily digested protein, and increased amounts of vitamins and minerals.

Consistency of feeding habits is essential. Because of the condition of the teeth, use softer, more easily digested foods. Include cooked oatmeal, grains or rice, cooked meat, glandular meat, cottage cheese, and boiled eggs.

Feed smaller amounts more often. For a change now and then, use any adult or puppy recipes that are soft and mushy.

DOGGY BURGER

(The Canine Dream)

Use equal amounts by weight of fresh ground beef, with white bread, whole-wheat bread, or pita bread.

Spread ¼" of the ground beef between alternate layers of bread.

Moisten with water or broth and bake for 1 hour at 300°F (150°C).

Allow to cool. But feed while still warm.

NOTE:

This is a great food for your dog when you take him on a picnic. Wrap the hot hamburger in foil and then several layers of newspaper. Feed at the same time you eat.

RICE PANCAKES

Use: ½ cup cooked white rice
2 eggs
½ teaspoon salt
1 tablespoon sugar

Beat the 2 eggs gently and add the ½ cup of cooked rice.

Mix the salt and sugar into the egg-rice batter. Stir everything gently.

Butter a hot pan and pour desired amounts of batter to make pancakes. Fry both sides until done.

Pancakes may be fed alone or mixed with other foods.

BREADED EGGBURGER

Mix 8 oz of cooked lean hamburger with one cup of bread crumbs. Add one scrambled egg. Mix everything well.

Feed warm without mixing with any other food.

MEAT TREAT SPONGE CAKE

Use: 1 lb. whole-wheat flour
1 lb. chopped lean meat

Mix the flour with enough water to make a paste. Add meat and mix well. Place in pan, cover with a cloth, and steam in the oven for 3 hours at low temperature.

Cut into sections and feed desired quantity. Refrigerate unused cake.

THE SOFT STARTER

Use: 4 oz raw brown rice
4 oz lean hamburger
1 chopped hard-boiled egg
1 teaspoon cottage cheese

Boil the hamburger in as little an amount of water as possible for 3 minutes. Drain and save fluid.

Mix hard-boiled egg, meat, and rice.

Add cheese and some of the warm broth to the food mixture. Feed warm.

THE SUNSET STEW

Use: 8 oz fresh tripe
4 oz chopped carrots, celery
4 oz fresh chopped liver
Salt

Wash tripe with cold water and drain. Place in a pot; cover with water. Bring to a boil, then simmer for one hour.

Add chopped vegetables and the chopped liver.

Salt to taste and simmer for another 20 minutes.

Pour off liquid and save for future use. Freeze if desired.

Allow mixture to cool and feed mixed with equal amounts of cooked rice or cereal grains.

THE PENSIONER

Requires: 1 raw egg
2 cups bread crumbs
4 oz chopped meat
4 oz chopped liver

Mix the egg with 1 oz of water and add to the crumbs.

Mix the meat with the liver.

Blend everything together.

Pour into greased baking pan, cover, and bake at 300°F (150°C) for one hour.

Cut into sections and feed warm.

A BROWN COW MILKSHAKE

Use as a treat for the toothless one. Mix 4 oz of milk with 1 very soft boiled egg. Add enough chocolate powder or liquid to give it a taste.

Blend gently together and serve warm.

THE ORGAN GRINDER

Use: 8 oz chopped brain
1 tablespoon white flour
1 cup bread crumbs
1 soft-boiled egg

Place brain in a pot and sprinkle with the flour. Cover with just enough water to boil and simmer for 15 minutes.

Mix bread crumbs and egg.

Drain brain broth and add egg-crumb mix to brains. Add enough of the broth to the food to create your dog's favorite consistency.

Feed while warm.

RICE PUDDING TREAT

Mix 1 quart whole milk with 5 tablespoons granulated white sugar. Add 5 tablespoons of raw rice and ¼ cup raisins.

Bake at 300°F (150°C) until milk is not visible—usually 3 hours. Feed at room temperature. Can be mixed with equal parts of canned meat dog food.

FEEDING THE WORKING DOG

Increased energy is the greatest single additional requirement for the working dog. For an animal to hunt birds, pull a sled, or race around a track requires stamina.

The metabolic rate in some of these animals is known to increase to the point where the dog requires four times the normal amount of calories. This high-energy requirement should be obtained from additional carbohydrates and fat in the food. It is also important that the B vitamin intake, especially thiamine and riboflavin, is increased as well.

The endurance of a working dog will increase if the dog is allowed to drink frequently. When you're out hunting, try to make provision for that.

Recipes in this book that are meant for healthy dogs can be used for working dogs during non-working periods. Foods used should be similiar to the ration to be fed while working.

Working dogs will require the extra energy whether they live in hot climates or cold climates. In cold climates the animal will compensate for this by increasing its food consumption by 20% to 25%.

In tropical climates the animal's food consumption is much lower than in cold climates. Quality of the food then becomes the compensating factor.

In either situation, if, during the working period, you use the same ration that you used during the non-working period, add:

- One tablespoon of vegetable oil for every pound of food consumed.
- 50 milligrams of vitamin C per day (in the form of sodium or potassium ascorbate).
- A vitamin supplement containing B complex and vitamin E.

If you own a working dog, it is well to keep in mind:

- That during non-working periods an acceptable level of exercise should be maintained.

- When working your dog, take a bottle of water and his water dish along. The endurance of the dog can be increased if the dog is allowed to drink frequently.

- Check your dog after each workout. Be sure to look between the toes and around the eyes for foreign matter.

- If it's necessary to ship the working dog by airplane, ask your veterinarian for a tranquilizer to keep the dog calm. Choose a schedule with the least number of transfers. During the summer try to use morning or evening flights. It can be very warm around airports during midday.

SAMPLE RECIPE FOR A DOG DURING A WORKING DAY

Boil 8 ounces of beef hamburger, in as small an amount of water as necessary, for 5 minutes.

Cook 8 ounces of white rice and mix with 1 chopped hard-boiled egg.

Drain the beef, but save the liquid.

Mix all the ingredients, excluding the liquid, and salt to taste.

Add a tablespoon of vegetable oil for every pound of food cooked.

Add a vitamin supplement that includes B complex and vitamin E.

Moisten the food with some of the warm broth.

Give 25% of the daily ration at least 2 hours before the dog works. Allow the remainder after work—1 hour or more later.

CATERING FOR A CROWD

FEEDING LARGE GROUPS OF DOGS AT ONE TIME

Whether you are feeding one dog or many, the same basic principle of good nutrition will apply. There is a difference when you feed an individual dog in a home and a dog confined to a kennel. The dog confined to a kennel has no chance for exercise. The quality of food should be maintained, but the quantity fed should be decreased. If the volume of food consumed remains the same during the period of confinement, then the amount of fats and carbohydrates should be decreased. Clinics and kennels should feed soft, moist foods in amounts correct for the size of the animal.

Confined dogs in strange quarters can be under stress as well. There are recipes and suggestions in this book for feeding special diets to dogs under stress.

While in the kennel, dogs must eat enough food to meet their caloric requirements. A palatable food will usually be accepted and eaten. Be sure it meets the nutritional requirement. Don't hesitate to add B complex vitamins as well as vitamins C and E.

Busy kennels should have a good variety of food in inventory. This should include:

- Canned dog food.
- Canned chicken cat food for new boarders that refuse to eat.
- Dry dog food that can be moistened with broth.
- Semi-moist dog pellets. Buy foods that claim not only a guaranteed analysis, but are complete and balanced. These foods can be added to your own recipes.

When shopping for dog food, buy bulk quantities of rice, mixed cracked cereal grains, and beef-based soup powder.

To save you the problem of cleaning dishes and to help stop the spread of disease, feed on pre-cut pieces of wax paper. In a strange environment, the appeal for the food seems to be greater when more food surface is presented.

Broths

Dry dog foods fed in kennels should be moistened with beef or chicken broth just before the time of feeding. Broths can be made with commercial concentrates such as Oxo or Bovril. Powdered beef or chicken concentrates can be used as well.

You can also make your own broths. Read the soup section of this book. Soups make wonderful broths that can be sprayed warm onto dry dog foods.

Food Mixtures

Canned and dry dog foods sell, depending on the area you live in, for 70¢ to $1.00 per pound. Rice and other grains sell for 30¢ to 70¢ per pound. The less expensive cuts of meat in North America sell for 40¢ to $1.25 per pound. A simple calculation proves that for "short keep" dogs in a kennel, blending your own food mixes is economical.

When preparing your own food, adhere to the rules:

- Cereals, rice or bread, or mixtures of them, should not constitute more than 70% of the total.
- Meat should be without bones and should not be more than 50% of the total.
- You can add a tablespoon of vegetable oil for every two pounds of food prepared.
- Cooked carrots and celery can be added in small quantities if desired.
- Vitamins and minerals can be added using label instructions.

TABLE OF EQUIVALENTS AND CONVERSIONS

3 teaspoons	=	1 tablespoon
8 tablespoons	=	4 ounces (oz)
8 ounces (oz)	=	1 cup
2 cups	=	1 pint
1 pint	=	16 ounces
2 pints	=	1 quart
1 ounce (oz)	=	28.35 grams
1 pound (lb)	=	0.4536 kilograms
1 kilogram	=	2.2 pounds

Room temperature is approximately 68°F or 20°C

To convert Fahrenheit to Centigrade:
$$C° = \tfrac{5}{9}(F° - 32)$$

INDEX

Allergies: about, 89; recipe for, 89
Amount to feed, 24
Apples, 105

Baby food, 81, 98
Bacon, 45
Bagels, 64
Beans, 16
Beef: about, 17; Baseballs, 51; Breaded Eggburger, 110; Broth, 123; Cowboy Casserole, 61; Diabetic Diet, 85; diet recipes, 102-103; Digestible Diet, 88; Doggy Burger, 109; for growing pups, 97; heart disease, recipe for, 78; kidney disease, recipes for, 83; A Liver Disease Diet, 87; Mother's Meat Soup, 39; with Rice, 51; Tea, 37. See also Hamburger; Meat
Bones: flat, 99; rawhide, 99
Bovril, 123
Brains: about, 17; Breaded, 74; Chopped, 114; Floured, 74; Fried Omelet, 48; how to cook, 73; The Organ Grinder, 114; The Scatterbrain, 48; Scrambled, 74
Bread: about, 19; Doggy Burger, 109; kidney diseases, recipes for, 83; mixing with other foods, 124; pita, 109; Snappy Biscuits, 65; A Standard Meal, 54; Sweetbreads, 72
Bread crumbs: Breaded Eggburger, 110; Mean Cuisine, 54; The Organ Grinder, 114; The Pensioner, 113
Breakfasts, All-Day, 44-48
Broth: about, 123; beef, 123; chicken, 105, 123; German Shepherd Meat Pie, 58; Ocean, 38
Buttermilk, use of, 32

Calories: content, 106; counting, 104
Canned dog food: about, 20; amount to feed, 24; for group feeding, 122; Rice Pudding Treat, 114; for special diets, 21; Standard Fast Food, 52. See also Dog food, commercial
Carbohydrates: requirements, 13; sources of, 14
Carrots: about, 16; Cowboy Casserole, 61; in diet recipes, 102-103;

measuring, 35; mixing with other foods, 124; Sheepdog Lamb Stew, 60
Casserole, beef, 61
Cat food, chicken, 32, 122
Celery: about, 16; A Diet Recipe, 102; mixing with other foods, 124
Cereals: about cooking, 27, 35; as dog food, 19; for group feeding, 122; mixing with other foods, 124; Rice Mix, 28; A Standard Meal, 54. See also Cornflakes
Cheese: as dog food, 18; Macaroni 'n', 52; Mean Cuisine, 54
Chicken broth, 123. See also Poultry
Coat, problems of. See Skin and coat problems
Consumption, average, 24
Conversions, table of, 125
Cookies, 62-65
Cornflakes, 50
Corn meal, 34
Cottage cheese: in bland recipe, 81; in diet recipe, 103; as favorite, 18
Cream of Wheat, 81
Crowd, catering for a, 120-24

Diabetes, 85
Diarrhea, recipes to combat, 80-81
Diet: changes in, 34; general information about, 12-24
Dog food, commercial: about, 20-21; labeling of, 21-22. See also Canned; Dry; Semi-moist pellets
Dog food, temperature of, 31
Dog meal. See Dry dog food
Dos and Don'ts of Feeding, 30-35
Dry dog Food: about, 20; amount to feed, 24; A Big-Hearted Recipe, 68; Boiled Beef Tongue, 71; Floured Brains, 74; German Shepherd Meat Pie, 58; Gestation and Lactation Diet, 93; for group feeding, 122; Kidney Stew, 70; as meal, 33; Scrambled Brains, 74; Sheepdog Lamb Stew, 60; Standard Fast Food, 52; Sweetbreads, 72

Eggs: about, 18, 31, 33; Bacon 'n' Eggs Breaded, 45; in bland

126

recipes, 81; Breaded Eggburger, 110; A Brown Cow Milkshake, 113; Chopped Liver Treat, 56; Kiddies' Cookies, 64; Layer Cake, 47; The Liver Best, 42; Liver Omelet, 46; Mean Cuisine, 54; Rice Pancakes, 110; The Scatterbrain, 48; Scrambled Brains, 74; Scrappy Omelet, 47; Slurpy Joe, 98; The Soft Starter, 111
Entrees, 49-62
Equivalents and conversions, table of, 125

Fast food, 52
Fat, bacon, 13, 14, 31
Feeding, consistency of, 31
Fish: about, 18, 30; in bland recipe, 81; as puppy food, 98, 99
Flour: white, 19, 64; whole-wheat, 19, 58, 111
Foods, mixing of, 23, 124

Game: about, 17; roasting, 29
Garlic rings, 17
Goat's milk. *See* Milk
Groups of dogs, feeding. *See* Crowd, catering for a

Hamburger: Breaded Eggburger, 110; Complete Macaroni Dinner, 53; Layer Cake, 47; Macaroni 'n' Cheese, 52; for older puppies, 99; for skin and coat problems, 84; The Soft Starter, 111; Stress Recipe, 86; for working dogs, 119. *See also* Beef; Meat
Hash: The Energizer, 51; Leftover Hash Cake, 60
Heart: about, 17; A Big-Hearted Recipe, 68; Heartbreakers, 67; A Small-Hearted Recipe, 68
Heart Disease: about, 77, 79; recipe for, 78
Horseflesh, 17, 103
Hot dogs, 55

Ingredients, common, 25-35
Intestinal disorders. *See* Stomach and intestinal disorders

Kidney disease: about, 82; recipes for, 83

Kidneys: about, 17; Broiled, 69; Stew, 70

Labels, reading of, 35
Lactation: about, 92; diet for, 93
Lamb, 60
Leftovers. *See* Scraps
Lettuce, 16, 33
Liquid, high-protein, 93
Liver: about, 17, 34; bland recipes using, 81; Chopped Liver Treat, 56; The Liver Best, 42; Omelet, 46; The Pensioner, 113; Sandwich, 42; substitution for, 67; The Sunset Stew, 112
Liver disease, 87
Lung, 17

Macaroni: 'n' Cheese, 52; Complete Dinner, 53; Mean Cuisine, 54
Meat: about, 17, 29; Beef Tea, 37; Chuckwagon Stew, 59; Complete Macaroni Dinner, 53; The Energizer, 51; Gestation and Lactation Diet, 93; Layer Cake, 47; Mean Cuisine, 54; mixing with other foods, 124; Mother's Soup, 39; The Pensioner, 113; Pie, 58; Ralph's Grill, 46; A Standard Meal, 54; Treat Sponge Cake, 111; *See Also* Beef; Chicken; Hamburger; Lamb; Mutton; Organs; Pork; Scraps
Medicines, giving, 90
Milk: cow's 96; goat's, 96; High-Protein Liquid, 93; powdered, 35; Rice Pudding Treat, 114; shake, 113; Slurpy Joe, 98; soy, 32
Minerals: mixing with food, 124; requirements of, 13; sources of, 15
Mutton: about, 17; allergy recipe, 89

Nursing bitches, 91-99
Nutritional requirements, 35

Oatmeal, 97
Oats, rolled, 34
Obesity: about, 101; recipes for, 102-103
Oil, vegetable: about, 31; mixing with other foods, 124
Older dog, feeding the, 107-114
Omelet, *See* Eggs

Organs: about, 17, 29, 332, 66-74; spleen, 17, 34, 67; sweetbreads, 17, 72; tongue, 71; tripe, 43, 57, 112. *See also* Brain; Heart; Kidneys; Liver
Overfeeding, about, 30
Overweight problem, the, 100-106
Oxo, 123

Peas, 16
Pills, giving, 35
Popcorn, 105
Pork, about feeding, 17, 30
Porridge. *See* Oatmeal
Posterior, problems of, 88
Potatoes: about, 16; Cowboy Casserole, 61; Dachshund Wieners, 50; Leftover Hash Cake, 60; peels, 32; Sheepdog Lamb Stew, 60
Poultry, 39
Powder, skim-milk, 35
Pregnancy: about, 92; diet for, 93
Pregnant and lactating females, 91-99
Protein: requirements, 13; sources of, 14
Puppies: frequency of feeding, 95; growing, 97-98; older, 99; orphan, 94-96

Quantity, cooking in, 34, 120-24

Rabbit, 17, 30
Raisins, 33
Recipes, combining, 23
Rice, brown: about, 19, 26; The Soft Starter, 111
Rice, white: about, 19, 26, 122; allergy recipe, 89; Baseballs, 51; Boiled Beef Tongue, 71; Cereal Mix, 28; Diabetic Diet, 85; digestible diet, 88; in heart disease recipe, 78; in kidney disease recipes, 83; Kidney Stew, 70; in liver disease recipe, 87; mixing with other foods, 124; Pancakes, 110; Pudding Treat, 114; Standard Fast Food, 52; Stress Recipe, 86; Typical Recipe for Skin and Coat Problems, 84; in working dog recipe, 119

Salami, 17
Salt, iodized, 15
Sandwiches, 41-43
Sausage, 50
Scraps: about, 19; German Shepherd Meat Pie, 58; Gourmet Canine Cookies, 63; Leftover Hash Cake, 60; Macaroni 'n' Cheese, 52; Poker Night Pig-Out, 55; for puppies, 31; Ralph's Grill, 46; Scrappy Omelet, 47; Standard Fast Food, 52
Self-feeding, about, 31
Semi-moist pellets: 21, 122
Sick animal, feeding the, 75-90
Skin and coat problems, 84
Soup: 36-40; Beef Tea, 37; Chicken, 33; Mixed Vegetable, 40; Mother's Meat, 39; Ocean Broth, 38; powder, 122
Spaghetti, 55
Spleen. *See* Organs
Stew: Chuckwagon, 59; Lamb, 60
Stomach and intestinal disorders: about, 80; recipes for, 81
Stress, 86
Sugar, 64
Sweetbreads. *See* Organs

Tea, beef, 37
Tongue. *See* Organs
Tripe. *See* Organs

Vegetables: about, 27, 33; A Big-Hearted Recipe, 68; Boiled Beef Tongue, 71; Chuckwagon Stew, 59; Complete Macaroni Dinner, 53; A Diet Recipe, 102; low-calorie treats, 105; Mixed Soup, 40
Vitamin-mineral supplements, 30
Vitamins, about: 13, 122; mixing with other foods, 124; sources of, 15
Vomiting, recipes to combat, 80-81

Water, 15, 30
Wieners, 50
Working dog, feeding the, 115-19